When You Give A Woman the World

A Travel Journal for Women

C. E. Fitch

Green Heart Living Press

When You Give a Woman the World: A *Travel Journal for Women*

ISBN Paperback: 978-1-954493-27-8
Cover artwork and design: Barb Pritchard and Teresa Hnat

This is a work of nonfiction. The events are portrayed to the best of the author's memory. While all the stories in this book are true, some names and identifying details have been changed to protect the privacy of the people involved.

This World We Share by Mark Weiss

Dedication

For Doug A. Stellato

My Biggest Adventure and the Love of my Life

Acknowledgments

To **Dr. Cyriac Pullapilly**, who saw potential in me as a college student and bestowed one of the coveted 'Semester Around the World' spots in 1999. This started the globe-trotting fever and accumulated the lion's share of the countries to which I have traveled. I can never repay him for his courage in leading so many of us challenging young souls to adventures untold.

To **Dr. Thaddeus ("Ted") Figlock** who has been a guiding light to me over the past 20 years:

-In medicine, as a retired Ob-Gyn he has positively influenced so many families.

-In faith, as a staunch Catholic he has prayed for me and my growth, reminding me of the narrow path.

-In radio, as my first contact (Call sign W1GHY) from the University of Notre Dame on our celebration of 100 years of radio in North America. Our friendship was divinely planned. It was Dr. Ted who talked me into writing down my travel memoirs, so you only have him to blame!

To **Dr. Albert Schweitzer**, my first global health hero. I admire that he was a master of many trades and a man of great spiritual depth. He was a pioneer with vision and convictions he shared bravely with a world generally not aligned with his calling.

To **Dr. Matthew P. Jones**, who shared my first international jaunt and was the one who got my parents' permission for me to travel abroad for a semester.

To my parents, **Charles and MaryAnn Fitch**, who were the first funders of my international adventures. My shortwave radio has been on every international trip with a listing of local stations, which I owe to my Dad. Thank you for giving this woman the world. I will never forget the treasure that you have afforded me.

To **Eric Nazarian**, the friend who can anticipate my every word and decision, perhaps because he has saved every word I've ever written on my global travels. Actions speak louder than words - your repetitive 'gifting' of my compiled travel journal emails after each trip gave me the confidence to share these stories.

To **Elizabeth Hill**, my life coach and publisher extraordinaire. Without your experience and support in the process, this volume would never have been completed.

And to my devoted friends who cared enough about these stories to give constructive feedback: **Jenn Hart, Matt Dausey, Gabriele Popp, and Sharon Beauchemin.**

I rest on the shoulders of giants!

Table of Contents

Introduction

This journal is for you! Give yourself time and space to dream about, record, and remember your adventures! The stories enclosed are to entertain and inspire, but not to eclipse your own mission of going forth and making your own memories. My travel memoirs span 20 years, representing many different chapters of training and growth as I became a world traveler and global health physician. Some names were changed to protect privacy.

Auntie Mame said, "Live! Life is a banquet, and most poor bastards are starving to death!" My hope for you is that you fill this life with interesting travel companions, jaunts along the unbeaten path, and sunrises that will connect you more deeply to the Divine. Rosalind Russell, my favorite actress who chose to star in the role of Auntie Mame, once said, "Taking joy in living is a woman's best cosmetic." Revel in your beauty, Dear One, and explore all the gorgeous facets of yourself as you joyfully journey through this awesome world.

Remember, every adventure has its moments of breathlessness, whether in panic or in awe, but it is all worth it in the end. No matter what happens, you will have a story to tell.

I say, *When you Give a Woman the World*, she can accomplish whatever her heart contemplates! LIVE!

First Step and Last Stumble

The sun rose over the tarmac. I sat in silent anticipation. As a college student, my whole life was in front of me. My father, the most important person to me, was with me from before dawn that day, probably more anxious than I ever could be. And it was a miracle I had even gotten to this point.

For weeks, I had been preparing for my semester around the world: 14 countries and 4 1/2 months with 30 other students. I was flying to Chicago where I would meet the other students and we would begin our travels together, starting in Japan. It was to be the adventure of a lifetime and I wanted it with all my heart. However, it had seemed that the odds were stacked against me. As a premed major at Notre Dame, it was difficult to go abroad at all.

The only sanctioned activity was a semester in England in the spring of one's junior year. That sounded so bleak - pubs and bangers and mash!

Why would I replace a semester at Notre Dame taking a trip that I could replicate at some other time in my life? And what would I gain from a culture that was so near to my own? This perspective may seem very privileged, and it was. Seventy-five percent of all Notre Dame undergrads go abroad for at least one semester during their four years. We were living in a bubble amidst the cornfields of privilege and, recognizing that, I wanted to expand my horizons and challenge my worldview.

As an anthropology double major, I wanted to experience various cultures. I looked into the abroad experience in Greece, but Athens had been riddled with violence in the year prior and that program closed. I ended up being able to travel to Greece on my semester around the world, but as it was all unfolding, I had no idea that could take place. I had looked into Haiti, but riots had made it too unsafe for students to travel there. I heard of a program from a guy who was in folk choir with me that sounded audacious. It was through St. Mary's College across the lakes. A history professor, Dr. Pullapilly, would be our guide to the world. I went to the informational session and was so intrigued.

During the fall break of my junior year, I came back to Connecticut to my parents. Neither of my parents traveled out of the country in their lives, though my mother was born in Hawaii at a time prior to it becoming a state. Somehow I did not feel that they would be receptive to my idea of a semester abroad. But I knew that this was my path and I was willing to put my neck out for what I wanted. I asked my parents to set aside some time when we three could discuss an opportunity for me, but there never seemed to be a good moment to talk. Finally, at the end of the vacation I told my mother that I had something very important to discuss with her.

I had recently been on a spiritual retreat that had been eye-opening and powerful. When I said to her that I had something important to discuss, she immediately burst into wracking sobs with tears rolling down her face and gasping breaths. I was stunned and dismayed, asking her what was the matter. She stammered out that she just knew I wanted to be a nun, but that meant to her that she wouldn't have grandchildren and she couldn't accept this.

With relief, I responded, "I just want to travel around the world."

Within seconds the deluge of tears had somehow dried up. And her response was, "Ask your father."

Surprisingly, Dad was harder to convince. He said that if someone had told him during the Vietnam War that his older daughter would be carrying a gun - she was in the Connecticut Air Guard - and that he would be paying for his younger daughter to go to Vietnam, he would never have believed it. He thought the whole situation sounded very dangerous. I tried to convince him by sharing that the cost was actually no different than a semester at Notre Dame for tuition. I expressed repeatedly how much I wanted to have this experience and how much I felt like it was important to my growth. It was actually my best friend, Matt, who reasoned with him that the University of Notre Dame would not sponsor a trip that would put students at risk of harm. I was shocked but thrilled that my Dad was on board with me traveling around the world from that point on. Matt also offered me some sage advice before embarking on my travels that has stayed with me to this day: It is a wise woman who inspects the toilet for snakes or insects before sitting down.

Over the weeks of preparation, my cat Lizzie spent more time in my one 40-pound backpack than any clothing or toiletries. All of a sudden there I was waiting to get on a plane to start my months of travel. Chicago where I would meet the other students and we would begin our adventure together, starting in Japan. I remember thinking how incredibly blessed I was to have a father who supported my dreams. In those days, 1999, I did not have a cell phone and there certainly was no option to get an international cell phone. We knew emails back-and-forth would be few and far between. My father would often send typed letters via fax to the next hotel on our itinerary around the world. And those letters were my lifeblood.

I was stretched emotionally and physically as we spent a handful of days in multiple Southeast Asian countries, touring world heritage sites at a breakneck pace. We crisscrossed the vast expanse of the diverse country of India, experiencing all climates from the Himalayan foothills to the coastline to the rainforest. When we settled in Cochi, Kerala, for our university studies, it was a relief. But before I knew it, the last three weeks of the semester arrived and we were touring Europe.

At the very end of the trip, in France, I became sicker than I had ever been in my life. The hostel in Chartres probably has still not recovered from my projectile vomiting and copious diarrhea. My travel companion, Karen, was also sick but with a respiratory infection. The two of us barely slept between bouts of illness and then the next day, like zombies, we made our way back to the Charles de Gaulle airport in Paris, leaving for home a week earlier than expected. We waited in the airport for about 12 hours on standby until almost midnight when we boarded the plane at the last minute. I remember all I ingested for those 24 hours was flat 7Up.

I didn't have a way to reach my father until we arrived at JFK in the wee hours of the morning. I called my father from a payphone to ask him if he would be able to pick me up from the bus stop in Connecticut if I could get there from JFK. He was startled awake and only picked up when he heard my voice on the answering machine. He assured me that he would be happy to pick me up and just wanted to be sure that I was OK. He told me later that when he hung up my mother asked him, "Who was that?!" "Christina," he answered. "Christina who?!?" was her reply since she could have never anticipated I would want to come home early.

I spent the next week recuperating at home on a liquid diet and wrapping up all the oddities I had shipped home for my family from different countries. My treasure trove included cloisonne Christmas ornaments from China, a marble plate with jasper and lapis lazuli made by artisans near the Taj Mahal, a batik shirt from Malaysia, and sandalwood fans from the Himalayan foothills. For my graduation gift to my parents in May of 2000, I chose the images of me that showed my metamorphosis over that semester and printed them on a poster in thanks for giving this woman the world.

First Step and Last Stumble
Self-Discovery

1. Do you enjoy beginnings or endings more? Why? Imagine yourself at the beginning and then the end of a journey and what you would say to yourself you hoped had shifted in that time.

2. Why do you travel? What adventures and what challenges do you envision?

3. Have you ever had someone keep you from reaching a goal? (or disagree with a decision you made?) How did that feel? What did you do? What lessons did you learn?

Elephant Blessings

India

I had not interacted with elephants before my 21st year of life, and I haven't since. But, during that very eventful year I had three experiences with elephants, all in India. The first special interaction was at the Red Fort in Delhi, which is highly frequented by tourists. There are elephants kept at the gates who, in exchange for a tip, will bless you with a tap on your forehead with the tip of their trunk. I felt bad for the elephants as they are held captive and made to live in the city, but I recognized that my money would hopefully contribute to their care and feeding. So, like many of my travel companions, I paid for a blessing.

I don't know if this elephant inhaled some of my long hair or if the great Divine was trying to tell me something about karma. However, when the elephant dipped its trunk down to give me a blessing, it sneezed all over me. I was covered with snot on my head and my arms. This was an extremely unpleasant feeling. That area is windy with lots of dust that stuck to the goop. I was like a walking fly catcher.

The second encounter was also in Northern India, on the approach to the Amber Palace in Jaipur. Rather than walking up the hill like any typical modern person, I decided to pay to ride an elephant on a palanquin like one might imagine the Maharanis of old. I had only been on horseback once in my life and that seemed a long way from the ground. Being on the back of an elephant feels like an unfathomable distance to drop to safety. The palanquin is set on the back of the elephant with only a strap around its belly to hold you secure. There are four people in the palanquin, each sitting on a corner to balance the saddle. The gait of an elephant dips quite dramatically as each leg moves independently. So every fourth dip, my life flashed before my eyes, thinking that the entire mechanism was going to send me crashing to the dry packed red dust.

My last encounter with the pachyderms of India was in the southern region at the rice paddy estates of my professor, Dr. P, who led us around the world. Dr. P rarely got home to his elderly mother and the estate on which all his earliest memories had been made, so he was so joyful to be with family. We all sensed his relaxation and really enjoyed our time on the grounds.

One of his brothers took one of the elephants which was used for heavy labor, such as moving tree trunks around the paddies, and entertained the group of students. Three of us decided that we were eager to mount the elephant's bare back. One of my companions got on first and called down to me how excited she was to be so high up off the ground. I clearly had not learned my lesson from the other two elephant encounters, because I was as eager as she was to try something new.

The elephant put out his leg for me to step on his knee and clamber onto his back. As I swung my leg over his very broad back, I heard and felt my pants rip up the center seam. Those pants had been washed by hand in bathtubs in at least six other countries over the last month. My legs were splayed so wide over this very thick elephant like I was doing a split that my pants apparently gave up the ghost. I enjoyed the harrowing ride with a breeze up my backside, then dismounted with a lot less grace. Three is a charm and my elephant adventures were complete.

Elephant Blessings
Self-Discovery

1. Have you ever tried something new that was scary or way out of your realm of daily living? How did you overcome your fear? How did you get the most out of your experience?

2. Have you had embarrassing experiences? How did you keep your sense of humor and dignity?

3. Have you witnessed animal cruelty? What did you do or how did you feel?

Sunrises

Malaysia, China, India, and Greece

One of the students that traveled the world with me had previously expressed her wonderment over sunrises. She cajoled a small number of us to share in her awe of dawn, leading us to some rather unique places, where we could bask in the light of a new day.

Our first sunrise together was on a small island of Penang, off the coast of Malaysia. On the night before our daybreak adventure, I found myself going to bed a bit earlier than usual. I was still convinced that I could tolerate some measure of alcohol despite prior experiences to the contrary. I had indulged in a substantial strawberry margarita at the in-pool bar. I had barely gotten myself back to my hotel room when my experiment began to produce its effects. I remember laying sprawled on the bed staring up at the ceiling, feeling as if the bed was twirling around in one direction, and then mercilessly changing direction and spinning the other way. I had never had vertigo before, so I was grateful when sleep overcame me as the effects of heat, sun, and alcohol combined. The next morning, I was up early and incredibly no worse for wear, able to attend our inaugural sunrise with my friends. The imam was calling from a far minaret as we made our way to the beach and the light grew into existence. The smell of jasmine dancing on the air was intoxicating, the calming sea breezes whispered to my skin, and the glittering dawn light on the waves dazzled the eyes. It was an incredible experience that I will never forget.

Our next sunrise together was a very different experience in Tiananmen Square. By then we had formed a merry little band of six or seven members. We became known as "those fools" - people couldn't understand why we would make the effort to get up at four AM to see a place by sunrise that we might already be touring during the day.

Tiananmen Square is a vast pavement reaching as far in all directions as the eye can see with a few temples around the perimeter and the mausoleum for Mao Zedong. Like the naïve students that we were from a Catholic university, we planted ourselves down in an open space and started praying and singing in a circle as the sun came up. Ironically, many of the group had bought red shirts with yellow stars for themselves, in an effort to find one another easily, especially in crowded tourist attractions. We did not seem to realize or care that the shirts were actually Communist symbols and antithetical to our spiritual beliefs. My friend who loved sunrises was also a songwriter. She had composed and taught us an *a capella* song. We figured that we would have a small and peaceful demonstration singing lyrics such as, "Jesus, break down these walls" and "take all my brokenness, rebuild me to shelter Your name." Though it was a small thing, it felt like a large statement: exercising our ability to worship, have free speech, and congregate peacefully. With the massacre occurring only 10 years prior, led by students calling for free speech, it felt quite radical and fitting. We were approached by some officials, but they left us alone after observing for a while.

Our next sunrise adventure together was at the Taj Mahal. We had traveled there as a group of 35 one hot afternoon. With so many people visiting the Taj Mahal every day, it was difficult to get such a large group in front of the monument without thousands of other tourists in the background, but we got it accomplished. Our small group was able to arrange for two carriages to bring us before dawn which provided a very different experience, the coolness of the morning offering a lovely change after the stifling heat and humidity of the days. The scam artists must have still been abed so we were not bothered by people offering to be in a photo and then demanding money for making the photo more authentic with a brightly dressed local in it.

When we got to the Taj Mahal, there were only a few other people there so watching the sunrise over both the Taj Mahal and the grounds was magical. The pearly light reflecting off the white marble was breathtaking and well worth the energy it took. We were able to spend much-appreciated time marveling over the semi-precious stone inlays and the architecture.

Finally, one of our last and most memorable sunrises together was in Greece. We had gone up to Mount Lycabetus using the funicular (cable railway car up the mountain) to watch the sunset over the Acropolis. But sunrise is best observed in the Parthenon looking in the opposite direction towards the Temple of Zeus, Roman Stadium, and National Gardens. It was born out again that visiting historic sites at sunrise is the best time to not be inundated with other visitors. One of our group brought his guitar so that we could commemorate the sunrise with a couple of songs, but he was chastised by the guard and told he was disturbing the peace. So, we ceased and desisted and just enjoyed the view.

I am sure 20 years later that there were many more sunrises that we shared together that were meaningful, however they have faded into the fog of memory. That trip taught me that it's worth the effort to enjoy a fresh dawn wherever you travel.

Sunrises

Self-Discovery

1. Have you ever gotten up early to enjoy a sunrise? What was the occasion? Was it worth it? What did you feel or remember?

2. It has been said, "you cannot step into the same river twice" (Heraclitus). Have you ever traveled anywhere twice where the experience was remarkably different? Where was it and how was it different?

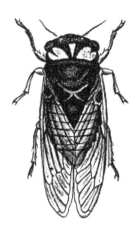

Insects Galore

Ghana

In graduate school, I went for the month of June through August for 12 weeks to live in two different areas of Ghana, first Accra, the capitol, and then to central Ghana, a village near Kumasi. The purpose of going to Africa for the summer was to study traditional birth attendants and their practices in order to understand why Ghana had a higher maternal and infant mortality rate than surrounding countries.

It seems that many people who have never been to Africa think that the entire country is the same, but this is far from true. There is a wider disparity between city and countryside in Africa than there is in the US. For example, one can shop at a grocery store in Accra, whereas all shopping is done in the market on market day in the countryside. And when one shops in the market, the entire town knows what you buy, therefore one cannot buy too many eggs or people will become envious because that is a show of great wealth. Most people cannot buy more than two eggs at a time and protein is more expensive than vegetables.

Another difference between the city and country is the amount, variety, and size of insects. Though there were cockroaches and spiders in Accra, many homes were fumigated and you did not encounter these as much. In the country, most of the floors were packed dirt with the occasional painted concrete floor and accordingly there was an increase in insects.

About a month into our research time in Ghana, we moved to the country to have better access to the traditional birth attendants and to work with a particular birthing hospital. We arrived late one night to a house without power. The rolling blackouts in the countryside were much more frequent than in the city. We were introduced to the insect population rather quickly. The locusts took one look at a visiting midwife's blonde hair with the bright reflection of the flashlight off of it and flew straight for her head.

I can only imagine how disconcerting it is to have a three to four-inch-long full-bodied flying insect come directly at your face in a house that only has one light source, a lantern flashlight. I was really grateful it wasn't me! Never was I so glad that

I am a brunette – blondes do not always have the most fun, especially when traveling. I had great compassion for my colleague who completely lost her cool, laughing in an unhinged way. I had never seen true hysteria, but this was surely it. In some ways better than screaming, this non-humorous high-pitched continuous laughter was just as eerie. It took her hours to stop, really not ceasing until she fell asleep. The only way that she could be convinced to try to sleep was agreeing to share a bed.

The large king-size bed had an equally large mosquito net over it. My colleague needed to have the flashlight lantern sitting on the bed between us with the light on all throughout the night. This became the norm for the rest of our stay in Ghana. It took me a long time to get used to sleeping with bright light right next to my face, but one can learn to accommodate almost anything. And it did help when one of us woke up in the middle of the night to use the bathroom that there wasn't a sudden bright light that went on in the room.

A couple of weeks into finally being able to sleep deeply at night, I woke up to screams in the bed next to me. I nearly hit the ceiling, or the mosquito net, as it were. When I was able to formulate words and asked what was wrong, she pointed up to the ceiling where the outline of a larger-than-life spider was displayed. My brain tried to make sense of this. I quickly realized that a spider has never been that big in Ghana. The lantern was casting a shadow of a spider that was on the outside of the mosquito net onto the ceiling. I realized this the moment before her screams disturbed the spider who jumped off the mosquito net to the floor and scurried away.

It was on a much-coveted trip to see the ancestral caves of our village that we had our final experience with country bugs. We only had one small flashlight in our vehicle. Knowing my trouble with seeing in the dark, my wonderful colleagues let me hold the flashlight. Once we had wound our way through the passages to the largest part of the cave, I was told to shine the flashlight down because we did not want to wake the thousands of bats sleeping at the top of the cave.

It had been very hot and humid outside and it was blessedly cool and refreshing in the cave. I was listening closely to the broken English of the guide describing how the ancestors would hide here in the cave during sieges from local tribes, losing my gaze in the copious bat guano on the floor. Suddenly, my heat-addled brain cleared and I realized that I was not seeing heat waves on the floor like one would see on hot asphalt, but that there was in fact an undulation occurring. It took a few more seconds as I scanned the beam of the flashlight back and forth to realize that it was in fact jumping spiders that riddled the floor of the cave. I spun around, grabbed each of my colleagues, pushing one and pulling the other as I screamed, "Get out!"

The guide rushed after us demanding to know what was wrong. We certainly were not acting like the expected foreign dignitaries who should feel honored by an ancestral cave tour. Outside in the bright light and the heat I babbled what I had seen... jumping spiders, all over the floor, you couldn't see because you didn't have a light. My colleagues started batting at themselves searching for spiders that had gotten up pants legs and skirts. We must have looked mad jumping around, very similarly to the spiders themselves. Yet, after so many other oversize and too close encounters with bugs in Ghana, no one became hysterical. We simply trooped back to the Jeep and refused to be coaxed back into the caves.

Insects Galore
Self-Discovery

1. Do you have any phobias? What would you like to avoid in your travels? How can you best prepare to avoid insects?

2. Have you ever been woken up suddenly at night? What were your first thoughts? How did you make sense of the situation?

3. Have you ever traveled with someone else where you had to accommodate their needs? What happened and how did you feel about it?

Oburoni

Ghana

In so many countries where I've traveled, I have felt like an outsider. But I think that there was a lot of value in living in Ghana, West Africa, for a summer. While I was there I gained a better understanding of what it feels like to be in the minority.

The colleague that I shared a room with was a very early riser and had showered and dressed before the sun was up. I, however, was not moving as fast in the morning due to poor sleep. I would do tai chi in the room, shower, and then dress before joining the others for breakfast. There were no blinds or curtains on the window, just bars. Every day, curious children and preteens would come by to observe the stranger.

The shower was literally a spigot on the wall in a closet-like structure with no door, so there was absolutely no privacy. I found it quite upsetting in a way to be watched in my ablutions and felt especially that it was not acceptable that the preteen boys should be watching me. However, they would not be chased away and the house staff could not understand why I was so upset, so would not do anything about it. They tried to explain to me that the children were just curious and wanted to see whether I was white all over.

After a time, I became accustomed to this voyeurism. as well as the children who would follow us to and from work screaming "Oburoni." "Oburoni" means foreigner in Fante, or "Those who come from over the horizon" (aka white person). We were the only two white people in the village so we knew Oburoni in any conversation referred to us.

About once every two to three weeks, we traveled into the nearest city to use the internet at the internet café to email our families that we were still alive, and to save our data by emailing it to ourselves. When we left the internet café, I spotted a white person *three blocks away* and whacked my colleague on the shoulder, shouting excitedly, "Oburoni!" I had no idea we stuck out like a sore thumb, like a neon sign in the night. Interestingly enough, my first thought was, what is that person doing here? She doesn't belong here. I was surprised that I didn't feel an instant solidarity with this person. Instead I felt that I was pointing out an incongruity or successfully identifying in one of those grade school exercises, there's something in this picture that doesn't belong.

Back in the village, we resumed our research with local traditional birth attendants and remained the only two Oburonis in the area. We had traveled from the States with a third colleague who was of half Ghanaian, half Nigerian descent. She learned Yoruba (Nigerian dialect) as a child and could understand some of the Twi around us and so was not seen as an outsider. During our 12 weeks, we faced a lot of challenges together.

My biggest challenge was the fact that we were called out to births mainly at night. I had not realized how poor my night vision was because back on campus I rarely walked at night and always where it was well lit for safety's sake. As I did not have a car in undergraduate or graduate school, I could not remember the last time I had driven at night. So, it took me by surprise that I would twist my ankles in potholes in the street and would conversely lift my feet high over small stones. It was made worse if I held the big flashlight lantern because my eyes would be blinded by the light. My colleagues finally realized my predicament after I nearly did myself a real harm and from then on, would walk arm-in-arm with me to and from the maternity hospital at night, each holding lanterns in their other hands. I was nicknamed "See no evil."

At the maternity clinic, the ladies would sing together and line up with their maternity cards so that we could measure their pregnant bellies and listen for fetal heart tones then dispense their prenatal vitamins. My midwife colleague who was also seen as an Oburoni was the favorite provider to listen for heart tones because it seemed to the local ladies very special to have this blond-haired lady to pronounce their babies healthy in the womb. The problem was that with the metal horns that we would press to the belly and hold to our ear, it was hard to hear anything. So, she would listen for long minutes and sometimes the mothers would become nervous. This colleague we termed "Hear no evil."

My other colleague developed a tooth abscess requiring antibiotics and multiple trips to the dentist in the city due to poor oral hygiene that summer. It was really difficult to use our precious drinking water for brushing teeth and it was that summer that I gave up wearing my retainer because I could never keep it properly clean, dooming me to braces AGAIN several years later. My poor colleague was on a diet of soft food for many days. We called her "Speaks no evil."

We finished our research two weeks early and the Oburonis tried to change our flights. It took several appointments, but we were able to get reissued tickets. Little did we know that every hand would need to be greased from the making of the appointment, to speaking to a Ghana Air agent, to finally stepping onto the plane. It took sponsorship from an influential doctor and hundreds of dollars just to return home. We made it back to the States where we no longer looked to the local people like

Oburonis, but our experiences that summer certainly made us feel like outsiders in our own skin. It was during my first dinner home, when I was sharing some of my stories with my family, that a hapless mosquito flew by me. I dropped my fork and clapped my hands over that mosquito so hard it never saw it coming. Both my parents jumped a mile and noted that I was now the "fastest bug killer in New England." I was happy to take on that moniker, certainly an improvement over "See no evil."

Oburoni
Self-Discovery

1. When have you felt like an outsider? Have you ever been uncomfortable with local customs? What are you willing to endure in terms of cultural discomfort for an adventure?

2. Have you ever made a connection with someone else based on your adversity or feeling like an outsider? What were you struggling with? How did that feel to know someone with a similar challenge?

Whirlwind Macchu Picchu

Peru

When one is traveling with 34 other doctors from around the world, it is not surprising that they are world-class travelers. I had taken a big financial risk and the opportunity of a lifetime to study tropical medicine in Peru. We cared for patients in three different regions: Lima (modern urban), Cusco (ancient urban), and Iquitos (rainforest rural). I was incredibly excited to go to one of the seven wonders of the world, but many of my colleagues had already been and decided to go to Huayna Picchu instead for mountain biking down that terrifyingly steep slope. A little gang of us first-timers chose to take the limited time afforded us to make the trip in a day. We were in Cusco to take care of patients with infectious diseases –

such exotic illnesses as leishmaniasis, cochlyomyia, and leprosy - and we were not afforded the five days needed to hike in and out of the region, nor were we given the three days most people use to have a more leisurely travel to and from Machu Picchu.

Altitude acclimation had not been without its challenges. Cusco is at about 11,000 feet and I remember waking up from sleep the first night and sitting bolt upright gasping to catch my breath. About three days in, when I thought I was over the transition, I found myself running up and down the two flights of stairs at the hotel five times before rounds at the hospital because I forgot one thing or another. I felt like my heart was ready to leap right out of my chest.

We woke well before dawn and took a cab to the bus station and a bus to the train station at Urubamba. As someone who regularly gets carsick in the backseat, the beginning of our day was fraught with challenges. I had found I did best when I ate nothing at all, chewed gum, and used Sea Bands. Even with all of these, it was still a trial. I think the fact that my mind was hazed with sleep may have improved the experience by fogging my memory with a sense of surreality.

The train was a really interesting and seemingly modern piece of machinery. The skylights at the top of the roof made it so that there was an almost panoramic view of the scenery. This was a lot of fun and made for a unique train excursion. I've taken Amtrak from

Hartford to Baltimore, rickety old trains around India, and even overnight sleeper cars from Switzerland to Italy, but this was a novelty.

We were getting excited that we were about 90 minutes from our destination and were sharing some snacks, when the train stopped. As none of us had ever been on this excursion before, we didn't know how many stops along the way there were or how long the train stopped at each station. After about 15 minutes of sitting still, we inquired of each other and other passengers what was wrong. This led to the reminder of how small the world truly is by meeting a fellow Domer (Notre Dame grad) on the train. As we waited, I played some card games with this gentleman and his three buddies who were also headed to Machu Picchu. It took about 30 minutes for a conductor to saunter through the car and tell us that we were going to be delayed for a while, but no explanation was given.

We were entertained by dancers and folklore storytellers who shared indigenous dances and tales to while away the time. One of these performers shared that there was something wrong with the engine (an alarming thought). Just when we wondered if we were going to spend the entire day on a stopped train, it started again.

I remember the scenery was very arid, which reminded me of Arizona, and quite desolate. Then the landscape changed to rolling green hills that reminded me very much of Ireland or Germany. When we got to the Machu Picchu station, I realized that the train does not bring one directly to the ruins. It stops at the base of the mountain in a town which seemed to solely exist to pander to tourists. Anything and everything with Macchu Pichu written on it could be acquired here.

Since we were running so late, we boarded a bus immediately that wound its way up the mountain in an incredibly switchbacked lane. Everyone held their breath as we veered to the edge of the narrow mountain road to allow the other buses to pass us, headed back down for more tourists. Looking back on all my travels, this may have been the most challenging day of motion sickness. At the top, my group of friends divided into those who wanted a guide and those who did not. I do not remember why I chose not to join the tour guide group, but I was very happy with my experience overall.

I spent a couple of hours wandering and exploring the open rooms and ruins, climbing as I pleased, and imagining life as an Incan. I went a little snap-happy, taking more than 300 photos, more than I think I have ever taken at any one place in my life. The overcast sky lent amazing light and contrast. I remember turning a corner after climb-ing up more stairs than I could count and there hanging on a precipice was a llama, itching itself with its hind leg, with the funniest look of ecstasy on her face. Such a moment of serendipity led to one of my favorite images from my entire time in Peru. I remember in the middle of the day, in the middle of the town complex, coming across a tiny bunny as he hopped across the open ruins, without any regard for the tourists. Though there were hundreds of people that day, the space was big enough and I was independent enough to spend most of my time alone.

Afterward, we met for drinks at the restaurant area outside Machu Picchu where I indulged in a nutrition bar and water for the crazy spinning trip down the mountain on the bus. Back at the bottom, we had about 30 minutes before boarding the train for the return trip back, so I lent some of my sol to the local economy and bought some kitschy gifts.

On the train ride back, the day caught up to most of us, and other than sharing some of the interesting anecdotes from the tour guide, most of the time we rested. Our bus ride home was eventful in that our little group squished into the small back bench of the bus. We were airborne more often than not on the bumpy ride, giggling madly in between bouts of exhausted silence since the intensely loud music did not allow for conversation. We got home very late at night, reeling from our visit to this ancient site bracketed by so many forms of transportation that made it possible to get there and back in a day. What a difference 600 years can make!

Whirlwind Macchu Picchu

Self-Discovery

1. How many means of transportation have you used in any one day? Have you ever experienced a dizzying disparity between modern life and history?

2. Have you been to a high altitude? How did it feel and what did you do to accommodate? Are there places around the world that you would like to visit at high altitude?

Good Day to Die

Peru

Throughout my three month stay in Peru, I watched the paragliders from numerous vantage points along the west coast of the city. From restaurants at Larcomar (the local mall) or Parque del Amor (the most romantic park in the city), I could see peaceful bright bits of silk floating on the breeze and would dream about how exciting and unique an experience that would be. Since the tropical medicine course that brought me to Lima was so intensive, I had resigned myself to not having time to try paragliding. But on my last day in the city, which happened to be Easter Sunday, I found myself at loose ends once my roommates left for their earlier flights. I reasoned that Easter Sunday would be a good day to die, if that was my fate. For an experience of a lifetime, it was worth the risk!

Since Peru is a very religious country, I was hoping that there would not be as long a line for paragliding as on other days, but luck was not on my side. I waited in line for over an hour, holding my completed liability form that put the responsibility of death or disability on me. When the gentleman who signed me up reviewed my completed form, he said that how I looked compared to what I had written down for my weight did not match. I told him that it was accurate in pounds, but he claimed that I was too heavy to tandem paraglide, and that the professional could not guarantee my safety. I argued that men who were bigger than me were going up tandem. I had to wait longer to find a larger Peruvian professional who was willing to take me up.

I had waited so long and my chance was so uncertain that when I did go, I paid extra to get GoPro footage of the trip. That meant I had to hold the GoPro handle and not drop it into the ocean hundreds of feet below. The anticipation and anxiety of being up in the air got me worried that my sweaty hands would lose grip, but I stubbornly decided that if I was going to go, I was going to record it.

Although my tandem guide spoke some English and I spoke some Spanish, communication was not perfect. The entire process was not explained to me before we took off. He told me to start running and keep running even when there was no longer ground beneath me. Fundamentally, what that means is you drop off the cliff and hope for the wind to pick you up. It was an act of faith to "run on air" and reminded me of the scene in Indiana Jones and the Holy Grail when Indiana Jones must take a step into thin air to get across to the cave that holds the Grail Cup. When the wind filled the sail, it was a truly exhilarating sensation. I whooped with joy and I could hear my guide chuckle in my ear. The wind currents off the cliffs are very predictable which is how the paragliding business at that location can run safely day in and out. We coasted on the breeze watching the cars on the coastal highway and the boats on the water below us. It was fascinating to experience what birds must feel as they ride along the wind currents and thermals.

When it came time to land, the tandem guide told me to "lift my feet" as we approached the ground. So, I brought my knees up but still had my feet touching the ground. Apparently, to drop the wind, you have to pretty much curl up into a ball with your bottom (the heaviest part of the body) hitting the ground. Since my weight shifted in unexpected ways, I heard my guide grunt and then exclaim some expletives in Spanish. It all happened in a blur, but I found us running back off the cliff again. As we were floating on the breeze a second time, he told me what I had done wrong, and then I told *him* how he could have better explained what to do!

There were no hard feelings, and since it was towards the end of the work day for him with few others waiting, we spent some extra time gliding before coming in for a perfect landing - the second time around. In retrospect, I "rose again" on Easter Sunday.

Good Day to Die
Self-Discovery

1. Have you ever done anything 'risky', such as paragliding, scuba diving, parachuting, or rappelling? Why or why not? What would you be willing to do for adventure?

2. Have you had miscommunication before with someone who does not speak the same primary language as you? What misunderstanding occurred? What would you do if you needed to communicate something to someone who spoke a different language?

Miscellaneous Massages

Mexico, Peru, and Vietnam

I've been an aficionado of massage for many years now. I started receiving massage after I met one of the spouses of a fellow resident at Dartmouth who was incredibly gifted and had the most wonderful spirit about her. She taught me how much my medical training had beaten out of me the ability to listen to my body. I found that massage helped me to reinhabit my body and it also boosted my immune system, which was helpful especially when I was working in the hospital.

In the United States, there is a general norm for the setting, preparation, and delivery of a massage. Lighting is usually low, either soft music or white noise is in the background, the temperature is usually warm, and sometimes a heating pad is used. Most importantly, modesty is maintained by keeping covered, except when a body part is being massaged.

I have sought out massage in several other countries for the cultural experience, but also due to therapeutic need as my body coped with challenging public transport, poor quality sleep, or lack of regular exercise. In Uganda, we used to joke that after enduring a long van ride to a patient's home for medical care, we had been provided an "African massage,'" since our bodies had been pounded and jostled on the terrible dirt tracks they called roads.

From the wretched resort massage that I received in Cozumel, Mexico while on a dive trip that left me feeling bruised and achy, to the Indonesian massage where I left slipping and sliding in my sandals due to the vats of massage oil rubbed into every square inch of me, they've all been tale-worthy experiences. But my favorite two were received in Peru and Vietnam.

About halfway through the intensive tropical medicine course I took in Lima, I realized that I was dying for a massage. One of my American colleagues was also interested in a massage. He happened to be fluent in Spanish whereas I was just able to get by. So, I was delighted when we visited the massage parlor together so that he could make the arrangements. I guess he wasn't as fluent as I thought because it turned out that he had booked a couples' massage. This meant that we were expected to be naked on massage beds in the same room undergoing massage at the same time. We were mature adults, and so decided that rather than forgo the opportunity to get a massage at a very good price, we would make the best out of the experience. And, we expected that, as in the US, modesty would be maintained by a covering while we were on the table. The massage therapists got a big kick out of the fact that I asked for a towel to cover me. What they gave me amounted to two face cloth-sized towelettes that I placed over my breasts and groin like an inadequate bikini. How mortifying to be lying on my back as good as naked next to my completely unclothed fellow American doctor! I had so many thoughts racing through my mind: could this be considered unprofessional behavior? What would his significant other think when she heard what happened? Would he even tell her? And how in the world did we get in this mess when he was supposedly fluent in Spanish?

My colleague and I agreed that we would just keep our eyes closed and attempt to enjoy the experience as much as possible. I have to admit that I never relaxed enough to get benefit from that massage.

The other highly memorable international massage experience was in Ho Chi Minh City. I was lucky enough to be visited by several friends during my six-month sojourn in Vietnam, teaching a fellowship in palliative medicine. One of those visitors happened to be my very first massage therapist! We thought it would be fun to exper-ience massage together as a way to relax and also to connect in the way that originally brought us together. There were some famous massage parlors that were run by blind massage therapists, but they did not have openings when we were looking for an appointment. Instead, we stumbled upon a parlor as we were finding a place to eat lunch and set up appointments for the afternoon. Similar to Peru, the therapist thought that since we scheduled at the same time that we would want to be in the same room. And, the cultural norm was to be completely naked during the massage. We decided that we would adhere to the maxim, "When in Rome, do as the Romans do".

We could never have imagined how hilarious the experience would be. When we got on the massage tables, there was no face holder, so we wound up staring at each other in close proximity. Our massage therapists were very petite Vietnamese women who, instead of standing on the floor, squatted on the table with their feet on either side of our body facing our heads. Squatting that long becomes difficult so they just sat down on our bottoms. My friend and I started laughing as we took in the absurd situation and the laughter shook the tables, making our massage therapists bounce on our bottoms. This of course made us laugh all the harder. We left that experience with our arms draped over each other's shoulders, totally united over one of the most ludicrous moments either of us had experienced. We reflected how different the experience was from our American massages and did wonder if native Vietnamese actually have a different experience, but the massage therapists thought they were giving us what we wanted.

I have received many massages since those two experiences, and I frequently recall them with a smile while I gratefully undress alone in the room and tuck myself under the protective blanket.

Miscellaneous Massages
Self-Discovery

1. Have you ever had a massage or some other personal care? What things happened that you think might be different in another culture?

2. Have you ever had your modesty compromised? How did you feel and what did you do?

Death by Motorbike
Vietnam, Uganda, and Indonesia

In Vietnam, I was teaching a fellowship in palliative medicine at a hospital. One of the stipulations of the six-month contract was that I could not ride on a motorbike. The reason for this was motorbike use amongst ex-pats is the fastest way to get killed in any country. This is especially true in Vietnam, where the traffic is almost exclusively motorbikes, the congestion is terrible, and there are very few traffic wardens. Death by motorbike is a common occurrence. Not only is injury on the motorbike an issue, getting to a hospital can sometimes be an even greater impediment.

I remember watching ambulances not moving in traffic for 15 minutes while they had their sirens running because they could not get out of a gridlock of surrounding motorbikes. What was astonishing was that the drivers seemed not to care. No one moved to the sidewalk or made any effort to change their course. I also remember being in an ambulance and almost getting into an accident ourselves. I was in the front seat not buckled as there were no safety belts in the vehicle. My two physician colleagues were in the back of the ambulance also without restraint. I saw that a vehicle had suddenly stopped in front of us and I was able to brace myself on the dashboard, but there was no time for me to shout a warning to my colleagues in the back. One went flying through the back of the ambulance, hitting her head on the metal door. She received a concussion.

My last day in Vietnam after all of my fellows had graduated (signifying that my job was done for the hospital), I decided to ride on the back of my interpreter's motorbike to have a brief experience of what it felt like to commute in Ho Chi Minh City. They were times I hung on for dear life and closed my eyes. Other times, I felt my knees brush against the legs of those passengers on the next motorbike over because the roads are simply so congested. I'm sure they could tell I was a foreigner because I was not wearing a mask or bandana over my face. Despite the heat, the women all wore long gloves and socks that were sown to be worn with flip flops so that not an inch of skin would be shown while driving. Heaven forbid one's skin should tan and make one look like a farmworker.

My favorite intersection was a rotary that I rode through to and from work every day that had at least eight lanes. In the middle of the road, ready to protect us all, was Kwan Yin. This female Buddhist deity, Bodhisattva of Compassion, looked so very transcendent and peaceful as the chaos of the knotted traffic around her untangled. Who is to say that she didn't help? I always got through in one piece.

In Uganda, motorbikes were a common mode of transportation, but the roads were not nearly as congested as Vietnam. One sunny day I walked down a long hill to the Friday afternoon craft market with a friend, not thinking about how I would get home. I had the intent of buying gifts for friends and neighbors to bring home since I was leaving soon. While I was there, I was captivated by the craftsmanship of the baskets and the vibrant colors. I left most of my clothes and toiletries in Uganda since there is such a need for all fundamentals even amongst those with full-time jobs. Two of my large suitcases were almost empty for the trip back home. With that abundance of space, I went a little crazy and bought 10 baskets to bring back to the states. A colleague had started the tradition of selling baskets back home to raise school funds for kids in Hoima, a very poor northwestern region of Uganda. So, I planned to sell these baskets and give the money to the same fundraiser.

The only way I could get back to my rented room back on the hospice grounds with my purchases was by boda boda (motorbike). I was grateful for the strong Portuguese thighs that I inherited because the ride back was harrowing! Since my hands were occupied holding the 10 baskets precariously balanced on top of each other in my lap between myself and the driver, I was pushed to the very edge of the seat. As we wound our way up a very steep hill with huge potholes that we veered to miss or large stones that sent me bumping in the air, it was only those strong thigh muscles that saved my life. I got off the bike very shaky indeed, but all 10 baskets sold in less than a day back home and the money was sent as intended, so the effort was worth it.

In rural Indonesia, where the topography was a lot less hilly than Uganda, we normally rode bicycles to and from the clinic, to get groceries, and to church. I will never forget the urgent call that the founder of the clinic and not-for-profit needed care herself. She had been stung by a box jellyfish a year prior and survived, which is miraculous. She had been evacuated to Singapore and then to Boston where she spent weeks recovering. When she finally returned to Indonesia, her nervous system was severely damaged and because of that when she went from laying to standing, she felt as if she was going to pass out. The clinic had motorbikes used for remote clinic visits and had recently acquired a donated handheld ultrasound.

The head doctor and I rendezvoused at the clinic and grabbed all the supplies that we needed in a flash. Ultrasound, check – put in one pants pocket. Sphingnomanometer (blood pressure cuff), check – held under my arm in its little pouch). Pulse oximeter, check – stuffed in the other pocket. Stethoscope, check – tucked around my neck. Medicine for blood pressure, check, and thank goodness that I had brought her refills from the states – placed in another pocket. I hopped on the motorbike behind him since I had never driven one myself.

In this rather lenient Muslim culture it was still very taboo for two young single unrelated people of the opposite sex to ride together on a motorbike, but this was urgent. As we took off, my heart was pumping from our hasty preparations. In my imagination, I heard the Indiana Jones theme song in my head as we sped off to her house, filled with purpose and youthful zeal. With the aid of the ultrasound, we were able to find that she had very low blood volume and this was what was making her feel so bad. Armed with that knowledge, we were able to treat her immediately.

Death by Motorbike

Self-Discovery

1. Have you ever ridden a motorcycle (driver or passenger)? Was it for pleasure or a purpose?

2. What was your worst traffic experience? Can you imagine what it would be like to be transported by different means (van, back of a truck, motorbike, train, bicycle)?

Way to Tipperary

Uganda

Some people can boast of brushing elbows with the rich and famous. I consider myself much more honored to have gotten to know someone who reminds me of my hero, Dr. Albert Schweitzer. The founder of the not-for-profit I had come to work was a nun for 20 years before she came to Uganda. When I met her, she was in her late 70s and still very active.

I had heard that she was quite a character – extremely opinionated, eccentric. Well, I had a lovely evening with her and enjoyed every moment. She had invited me to her home since I was a visiting doctor donating my time and expertise. Perhaps we had such a good time because we shared the same strong opinions and perhaps I'm irascible too. We exchanged books: On my part "Dying Well" by my mentor Dr. Ira Byock, on her part "Cicely Sanders: The Founder of the Modern Hospice Movement," a biography about the woman who inspired her to work in palliative medicine. And my Bailey's Irish crème chocolates were a hit as a gift, which is always nice.

This most enjoyable meeting of kindred spirits started inauspiciously with me twiddling my fingers on the back porch for 30 minutes because she didn't know I had arrived. It was not difficult to figure out why she hadn't heard me come in. For starters, the biggest palm tree in the back garden about three feet in diameter had died and it was being cut up into stool-sized pieces with the loudest chainsaw I've ever heard. Only in Africa does the chainsaw burp out black smoke and three other men are needed to stand around pontificating on the hard work being accomplished.

In addition to that cacophony, one of the people who lives in the compound with this inestimable woman is a 12-year-old girl who was playing an Indian soap opera at supersonic levels, probably because she couldn't hear it over the chainsaw. On top of it all, the dogs were going mad over the intruders in their compound. The police force and the veterinarian were supposed to have picked up five of the dozen or so dogs that Dr. Anne had bred for security. But, just like everything else here, dates and times don't seem to matter much. If the dogs weren't enough, the cats were all meowing for their dinner. I think I had counted seven cats. Due to all the dust in the country, even the white of their fur looked brown.

I will never forget the moment, as my head is reeling from so much noise, that this white-haired woman in a mumu appeared around the corner. I had a difficult time making sense of her, especially since she was singing at top volume, "It's a long way to Tipperary" as she marched along doing her cardiac exercises. And her 18-month-old African 'granddaughter' Vickie was trailing along behind her. They were both carrying water-filled bottles, proportionate to their size, pumping them up over their heads and out to the sides as they marched up and down the veranda. It was really quite amazing that Vickie knew the whole routine, as little as she is, and could march along in her Jaja's (Ugandan Grandmother's) wake. I joined in for fun, uproariously singing a song to which I don't know the words and flinging my limbs about to mimic the calisthenic program before teatime. I cannot tell you how truly surreal this felt. Dr. Anne's housestaff make cakes for another source of income and the raisin cake they made was delicious. I had really worked up an appetite. But the conversation was yelled at top volume because all of the above racket never ceased.

It wasn't for a couple of hours over dinner that it quieted enough for us to have a normal conversation. I very much enjoyed my time with this lovely, authentic woman since we happened to share the same worldview. Before I left to return to the States, she gave me a wooden cross made in

Uganda that has the figure of Christ as the cross, the gnarls of the olive wood somehow conveying his suffering. I have kept it close by always, whether it was in my office at the hospital or now, at the entrance to my home. This physician and prior nun is a character for sure and I want to be just like her when I grow up.

On the way home, she called a private car for me. Steven was my driver and he was quite the philosopher politician. In 10 minutes, we had the world's problems solved. It is so interesting and invigorating to come across someone unexpectedly who hails from a world apart and with a very different upbringing, but with the same social viewpoint. It was my blessing that I had my life edified by two in one evening and got some exercise in, too, on the 'way to Tipperary'.

Way to Tipperary
Self-Discovery

1. Think about someone you've met who had a very different upbringing than you. What was it like to speak with them? How did your views differ or how were they similar? What did you learn from them?

2. Have you ever had a surreal moment when you wondered if something you were experiencing was real? What were the thoughts and emotions at that time? How did you respond?

3. Have you ever met someone where your first impression of them was very different from what you were led to expect? How did you reconcile the difference in your own mind and heart?

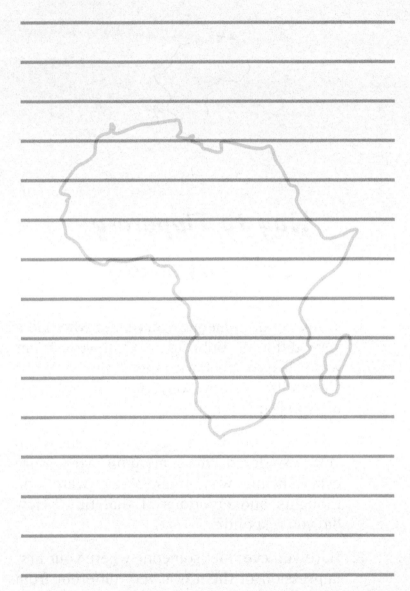

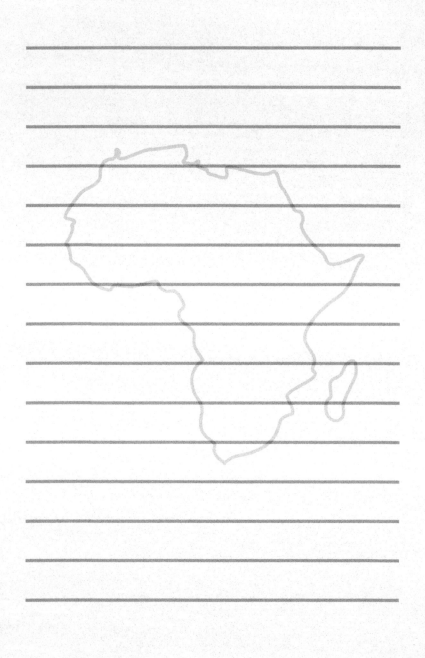

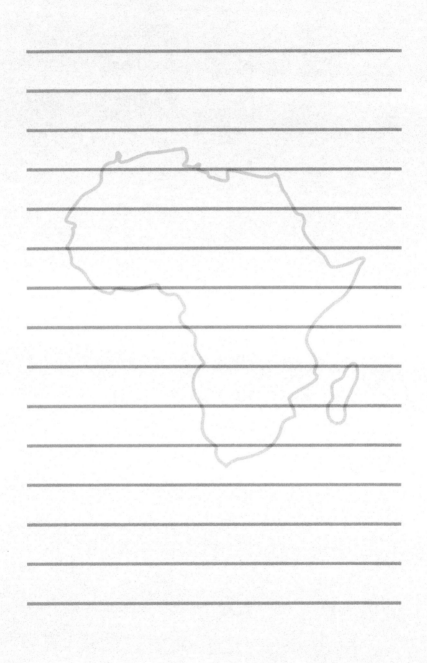

Explosives and Vegemite

Visiting Australia was a wonderful experience, but it was in the leaving of it that I found true excitement. I never imagined the mayhem and adventure that could be found in the Sydney airport.

A couple days before leaving Australia, my travel companion, John, had decided that in return for the lovely gift of snorkel, fins, and underwater camera that his staff had given him for our Great Barrier Reef visit, they were owed an equally exciting gift. After much deliberation, and against my vehement recommendations, he decided on Vegemite, a condiment that is unique to Australia. Few other countries tout this leftover brewers' yeast extract as nutritious and savory, likely because it is so foul that nowhere else in the world can sell it.

Despite not having bought much in Australia, neither of us had a lot of room in our bags for the dozen tubes of Vegemite that he had bought in the

Cairns airport. I could imagine all these containers bursting in our luggage under the dramatic pressure changes of multiple takeoffs and landings. Given this predicament, he decided to leave the containers in the original duty free bag and assumed he could bring it as a carry-on. However, he was sadly disappointed to find out that since he did not buy the Vegemite in that airport that it was considered too many ounces of liquid/paste substance brought from outside. He was told that he had to relinquish it before he came through security. In total he was attempting to transport about $100 worth of Vegemite, which is probably more than anyone in the world has ever bought at once or maybe even in their lifetime. This is likely why the customs officers thought it so strange that he was insistent that he wanted to keep hold of his precious Vegemite.

As John was arguing with the customs agents, I was also trying to get through customs. Since my travel companion was acting suspiciously, my hands were dusted for explosives. I cannot remember ever in my life being so alarmed as when the customs officer yelled out, "I HAVE A POSITIVE!". I imagine in her very dull line of work, this is likely the most excitement she had in a long time. My heart was racing and my palms were sweating; I'm sure I appeared guilty. However, in the back of my mind I could also see the ridiculousness of the situation and wanted to laugh inappropriately. The minute she shouted gleefully, several officers came running. I couldn't believe that two such seemingly ordinary people could cause such a ruckus. I told her that I had not used explosives ever in my life and that I thought it was a false positive, but she did not believe me.

After being interrogated for a while, the other officers urged her to test again. And again. And again. And it never came up positive. She was so put out that I had ruined her fun and angrily sent me through customs to meet my travel companion who had been waiting on the other side for half an hour, sans Vegemite. Later, upon reflection, it seemed likely to me that they had originally picked up some of the cream I had put on my wrist for tendonitis. There must have been just a little residue of the anti-inflammatory on my fingertips. Against my better judgment, my travel companion shelled out another $100 to replenish the ill-fated Vegemite, this time purchased beyond airport security, and we continued home to the States. "B vitamins for Vitality" may be the famous slogan, but we remained sadly deficient.

Explosives and Vegemite

Self-Discovery

1. What gifts have you bought or would you consider buying on your travels? Who would you get them for and why?

2. Have you ever had a friend make a decision that you didn't agree with? How did their decision impact you? What were the circumstances and how did you handle it?

Siem Reap
Temple Adventures
Cambodia

When in Vietnam, it is very convenient to take short flights to other Southeast Asian countries through Vietnam Airlines. I was lucky enough to have some four-day weekends and planned a trip to Cambodia to enjoy the temples. I was meant to rendezvous with a friend from the States, but that fell through at the last minute. It's amazing when you travel for long enough that friends of friends often are in the same place as you at the same time. Things often work out at the last minute, as in this circumstance, where friends of a friend were at the same hotel as me and I heard about their visit right before I embarked for Siem Reap.

I arranged for an evening food tour of the night markets before my acquaintances arrived. My guide was a lovely gentleman of middle age who had lived there all his life. He showed me many insects for sale in the market, including fried tarantulas and centipedes, which I graciously declined to buy. I had seen similar in Peru so was not as horrified as his average tourist, to his disappointment. I enjoyed watching some noodles being made by hand. And we went to a local bar and had soup and coconut milk drunk straight out of the shell. It was fun to ride on his motorbike with him around town like the locals, but none of it was all that novel to me.

I think it would have been a more enjoyable experience with a group because it became uncomfortable after he found out I was not married and did not have any children. Anywhere in Southeast Asia, it did not make sense to many people that I was an able-bodied young woman who chose to be single and had gotten this far through life without any of my own children. The analogy in the US might be if I were asked what I did for work and I answered nothing. In effect, it was a real conversation ender.

All three nights that I stayed in the lovely hotel I had vivid and colorful action-packed nightmares of death, destruction, pain, and suffering. In my memory of those nightmares, I remember a lot of red and black and screams of terror. I've really never had an experience like that anywhere else in the world where I slept so poorly and had such recurrent dreams. In fact, I rarely suffer from nightmares and when I do I usually wake with a feeling rather than visions. Instead, I woke multiple times each night and returned to the same dreams, which is also a novelty for me. I wonder if the violence that region has seen permeates the soil that the hotel was built upon and I sensed the unrest. I am not usually a superstitious person or one who believes that a place necessarily holds evil, but that experience was difficult to shake.

Also based on a friend's recommendation, I had scheduled a rickshaw driver to pick me up in the morning and be my tour guide for Angkor Wat. This temple expanse is absolutely stunning in its carvings and architecture. The history that is recorded pictorially and the spirituality that is represented by these images is extensive. There are simply no words to describe the wonder after visual wonder presented as you move from room to room. It is said to be the largest religious monument in the world and I felt incredibly blessed to spend time there.

The first day it rained intermittently quite hard. I felt like a drowned rat at times and certainly was not photo-worthy. The rain was coming down in torrents at one point and I saw a vivid blue Morpho butterfly on a branch that fell into a puddle below. I picked up the delicate Morpho gingerly, tried to find it a place of protection, and placed it back on the branch. I hoped the place I selected would allow it to dry its wings, not fall back into the puddle, and actually survive the deluge. I watched over it for a few minutes, getting drenched in the meantime and my feet becoming soaked through. But the utter exquisite beauty of this bright blue butterfly really touched my heart. I had never seen anything like it and enjoyed my brush with this ethereal being.

When the rain had stopped, I came across a small boy who played at a roadside stand where one of his family members was making caricatures of people. I didn't have the time to sit for a caricature, but I interacted with this preschool-age boy who held out his puppy to me. Neither of us spoke a common language, but it was clear that he wanted me to buy the mutt. He and the puppy were both so ragged and sweet in their innocence. I was completely drawn to them and wanted to take them both home.

I enjoyed my rambles through the temple complex thoroughly and my guide was very sweet. I imagined that the experience of these temples would have been so different when they were built hundreds of years before because they were in fact in color at that time. I can barely imagine the vivid hues extending over acres and acres. The austerity currently makes for wonderful photos in terms of seeing patterns or having your bright clothing highlighted against the drab backdrop.

Interestingly, in between rainstorms, I saw many Asian tourists in groups taking professional photos in crazy outfits. They did not appear to be magazine photoshoots, but bunches of girlfriends or families taking the images to commemorate the trip. It occurred to me that this would not happen in the States in a building that was historically a place of worship.

That afternoon I relaxed with a swim and chatted with the mutual friends also at the hotel. I was so worn out from poor sleep. The next morning I rose at 4:30 and got a cab to Angkor Wat, Angkor Thom, and Ta Prom. Once again, I felt that there was a coincidence of global travelers. As I was getting into my cab at the crack of dawn all alone, I saw two other tourists, Kiwis specifically, come out of the hotel. The window was open as I pulled away and I overheard the bellhop tell them that since they did not arrange for transportation to the temples the day before that they would miss sunrise by the time all was arranged.

I asked the cabbie to drive back around the portico and asked if they wanted to join me. They were delighted and it turned out to be much nicer being with other travelers. Between us and our guide books, we were able to learn some of the history. It was very convenient to have people to take photos with me in it instead of relying on selfies.

It turns out Angkor Wat at sunrise is swamped. I had to crouch down at a strange angle get a photo of me with the peacock entrance to the temple complex and the sunrise in the background without the hordes of people in the shot with me. I felt an unspoken bond with this large crowd of people from all over the world, as we appreciated this sunrise together at this ancient site.

I most enjoyed Ta Prohm, which is where Tomb Raider was filmed. The trees have disrupted the temple stones and their roots have become part of the structure in fascinating ways. One of the guidebooks explained that if the trees were cut away, the temples would fail, so the stones and roots give reciprocal support. This part of the complex felt more magical to me and other-worldly. By the time we had traipsed all over the temple and shared our mutual snacks, we had whiled away more than half the day and were ready to go back to the hotel and bask in the pool again.

I considered attending a musical evening in town, but could not figure out the transportation, ticket sales, and dinner arrangements without stress, so decided on a quiet evening catching up on emails. I had done what I had set out to do, steep myself in the history of this region. The thought of all those not yet detonated landmines still in the area also made me think twice about crossing the town. Instead, I went to sleep early and had continued intrusive and chaotic dreams.

Siem Reap
Temple Adventures
Self-Discovery

1. Have you ever had location-specific dreams? What were they about and how were they different from your regular sleep experience?

2. Have you ever toured a spiritual site? What did you feel? What were your favorite things or what do you remember most?

Giant Chopstick Spider Catcher

Vietnam

In Ho Chi Minh City in a lovely little first floor flat, I was lulled into thinking that I was living in the lap of luxury. Suddenly, I realized southeast Asian living is not complete without a large spider infestation.

Strange to say, I had become accustomed to the excessively large cockroaches, two to three inches long. Most mornings when I would turn on the lights and walk into the kitchen, I would come across at least one of these giants who had somehow flipped over onto their backs. I knew if they were dead or not if all their legs were still waggling in a desperate attempt to flip over.

But the spiders are a different story. Imagine a large hairy spider about the size of the palm of your hand. They moved so quickly that sometimes you couldn't follow where they had wound up if you blinked. They seemed to especially enjoy living in the lip of the decorative ceiling in the bedroom. Sometimes in the night, they would drop down the 10 feet to the floor, before scuttering off to the bathroom. I felt like Miss Muffet in the rhyme: "Eating her curds and whey; Along came a spider, Who sat down beside her, And frightened Miss Muffet away." The measures I had taken to try and get a good night's sleep while it was 'raining spiders' were a bit excessive and included moving the bed to the middle of the room, sleeping with the lights on, and spraying the room with bug spray until I could barely breathe through the miasma.

One fateful night, I was so sleep deprived from worrying about dropping spiders that I was strung out a bit beyond sanity. I must have been half asleep in my brightly lit up bedroom, when the largest spider I had yet see dropped from the ceiling onto the bed. I commenced screaming like a mad woman and thrashing at the bed clothes. The spider must have heard me or been disturbed by the earthquakes of the mattress, because he dropped to the floor and started running towards the living room. I tore after him thinking that I can corner him and kill him. The spider managed to get under the sofa in the corner. Before I could even think about my next move, the night watchman commenced banging on my door. He was hollering in Vietnamese, which I did not understand. I let him in because I recognized his voice. Through gesticulations and shouting in English at him, he understood the spider had scared me. He looked under the sofa and in the dark apparently saw this very large creature. And he ran out the door.

I was so frustrated and overwhelmed. How could he have lived here all his life and he's also scared of the spiders? But he came back a few minutes later with two large yardsticks. I looked at him in disbelief, wondering what in the world he meant to do with them. He smiled as if he understood my disbelief. I had underestimated this guru of utensil utilization; he truly had made it to the highest level of chopstick professionalism. He spent the next 10 minutes on the floor with those yardlong chopsticks underneath the sofa. I huddled in the corner watching in disbelief, but not being able to go back to bed until he left. Eureka! The night guardsman got to his feet in triumph and brandished the very large and struggling spider that was held in the pincers of the giant chopsticks.

I cheered and was astonished to hear myself yell, "kill the bastard!" Since the night guardsmen couldn't understand me anyway and he must have seen some worth in this very large spider, he took it outside to release it. This seemed an excessively ignorant thing to do since that spider clearly enjoyed living inside my apartment and had found its way in previously. And the horrifying cycle began again.

Giant Choptick Spider
Catchers
Self-Discovery

1. Have you ever had insomnia? What caused it? What were some consequences of not getting adequate good quality sleep?

2. Think of someone you may have underestimated. How did they surprise you? Were they aware of how you felt about them and the shift in your understanding?

I Think He's Dead

Haiti

Though there was 6 years between my visits to Haiti - 2011 and 2017 - very little progress had been made in reconstruction after the devastating 2010 earthquake. In 2011, I was blessed to go to Haiti as a personal physician to Dr. Emil T. Hoffman, professor emeritus at Notre Dame in biochemistry. He was a legend among legends at the university, especially for pre-medical students over a four-decade time span.

Dr. Hoffman was in his mid-90s and that was to be his last trip to Haiti to see all the people and places he had loved and supported over the years. He knew it and we knew it. What I was unaware of, was that he was a great man for many other reasons than teaching. He had supported the Notre Dame Lymphatic Filariasis (Elephantiasis) program, and had been a benefactor of the St Rose De Lima

Parish School and an orphanage near Port-au-Prince in the town of Leogane. Tragically in the earthquake of 2010, much had been destroyed. The principal of the school, Sister Esta Joseph CJ, who was his personal friend, had been killed during the earthquake. Two of the only buildings left standing amid the devastation housed the Notre Dame Haiti program. I had traveled with a group of doctors who were prior students of Dr. Hoffman over the years; he had led these reconnaissance trips for 17 years so that we could see how we could help on future trips.

Now in November 2017, I returned to Haiti on the other side of the island near Cap-Haitien for a different purpose. I traveled with a motley group consisting of surgeons, nurse anesthetists, OB/GYN's, and students, many of whom had traveled together before and some of whom were related. On the plane from Boston to Miami I was sitting separately from the rest of the team because I bought my flights separately. I sat near the front of the plane and struck up a very cordial conversation with a lady in her 50s who was going down to Florida for a work conference.

About two-thirds of the way through the flight there was a great disturbance behind me. Very shortly, there was an overhead announcement requesting a "Physician, STAT!" in the back of the plane. I quickly got up to help and got halfway back when I realized that my colleagues were already at work. I turned around and went back to my seat since there was no additional space to congregate.

The lady sitting next to me asked if I knew anything and I responded that there was someone who was ill in the back of the plane, but that they chose the right flight to get sick because there were so many physicians to help. She made a crack about hoping that this wouldn't turn the plane around. About five minutes later, the flight attendant came to get my seat companion, letting her know that it was her husband who had collapsed.

I later heard the story from my colleagues. The gentleman had collapsed in the aisle in between my close friend (surgeon) and her father (anesthesiologist). Also on the plane were my friend's mother, and cousin, both surgical head nurses. Quickly, my friend and her father assessed the man and found out that he was pulseless and not breathing. They did one round of CPR on him and resuscitated him without the defibrillator, which is nearly miraculous.

My friend's cousin screamed out "Oh my gawd, I think he's dead!" in her thick Boston accent. The back half of the plane was terrified when the man tumbled to the ground! I wondered why a surgical head nurse would lose her cool in crisis, but the operating room is one of the most calm medical settings with very few real emergencies. So perhaps it's not surprising that she almost incited a riot with her outburst.

What surprised me the most was that my seat companion and her husband lived just across the river from the hospital where we all work. The flight attendant came to console her and stated that she should not be surprised if her husband had chest pain after the chest compressions and that she should not worry or seek care for that. I was astonished that she would give medical advice in such a cavalier and uninformed manner. I interjected that if he had continued chest pain, he should be emergently sent to the hospital. I attempted to educate her that if his heart stopped beating once, it could very well happen again, and that he should in fact be hospitalized when they got down to Florida for a cardiac workup. Her plan instead was to leave him on the beach while she enjoyed her conference and allow him to recover. This was a great example of the lesson I've had to repeatedly learn, "You can lead a horse to water, but you can't make it drink."

It rained several days during our stay in Cap-Haitien and there was copious flooding in the streets. The most challenging day that week, it was pouring cats and dogs. We got into our two hired vans and barely made it down the very steep hill that our hotel precariously perched upon. There was a man at the end of the driveway directing traffic because the vans would just freefall down the driveway, slipping and sliding, unable to brake. I thought that the harrowing adventure was over once we reached the main street, but the shen-anigans continued. There was so much flood- ing in the main street because of poor sanitation and drainage, that our engine nearly flooded. We float-ed down the street until we could get to higher ground. We then had the 90 minute drive to the hospital where surgeries would occur all day long.

About halfway into our drive, we were stopped by large crowds. This is not unusual in Haiti and that year the riots were particularly bad. This demonstration was actually led by teenagers because the school roof was leaking so badly that they could not safely attend school. I never thought I would be afraid of school-age children, but the frenzy and tone of that riot was scary. The students were brandishing the chairs and desks over their heads and were in no emotional state to let strangers pass.

We realized after about half an hour of sitting in the van without progress that if we were going to get to the hospital at all that day we would have to literally walk straight through the riot and look for a tuk tuk (open-backed pickup truck that holds passengers) on the other side. We were all in scrubs so were clearly foreign medical prof- essionals and our Haitian drivers walked at the beginning and end of our single file snake as we weaved through the angry crowd. It reminded me of kindergarten when we were asked to hold hands and not let go so we would not get lost in crowds on a field trip.

My heart was racing and my mind was forming dire possibilities of what would happen if any of us were injured or taken hostage by one of the adults interspersed in the crowd. We experienced some pushing, raised voices and some menacing attention, but no overt violence. Thankfully, we made it to the other side in about five minutes. And, we were able to find a large tuk tuk to carry us the rest of the way to the hospital.

Surely the adventures were over, but once again no. I get very carsick, especially traveling facing backwards. The roads in most of Haiti and in particular in that area are very windy and steep. The tuk tuk needed to take sharp turns or tack across the road to navigate the many potholes. This weaving with acceleration and deceleration can really contribute to the motion sickness.

The only way that I was going to survive this trip without vomiting was to hang on to the back of the truck with my feet on the back fender and one hand wrapped around the grab bar, allowing the wind to blow across my face.

There was no tailgate or any other safety measure and the rain was still coming down in buckets, so all the metal surfaces were very slippery. It occurred to me that if either my hand or my foot slipped that I would likely die on the road and nobody would know that I was missing until they made it to the hospital. So, I held on for dear life, hoping that since I had already survived flooding and riots that my luck would hold through this last hurdle to safety. We all made it to the hospital and pulled ourselves together to complete the day's planned surgeries as the patients had waited months for the specialists to come to Haiti to treat them. We could not let them down. After the surgery, in my role as palliative physician, I helped them to start their journey to healing with less pain.

I Think He's Dead
Self-Discovery

1. Have you ever been concerned about your safety? How did you survive? How did you get centered again afterward?

2. Have you ever been involved with bad weather? Have you ever witnessed a medical emergency? What were the emotions during and after the experience?

Photos

Semester Around the World in Kerala, 1999

Elephant Blessings in India, 1999

An Oburoni in Ghana, 2001

On top of the world in Machu Picchu, 2013

Paragliding in Lima, 2013

Sydney Quay in Australia, 2014

Pretending to ride a motorbike in Ho Chi Minh City, 2014

Temple Adventures in Siem Reap (Ta Prohm), 2014

Live and Give Globally

Throughout my travels, I have found some large non-governmental organizations that did not use donated funds frugally or ethically. In contrast, the organizations listed below are ones where I know the founders, have been on the board, have worked in country with them, or have felt their model is so exemplary that I have presented at medical society meetings about them. Suffice to say, I trust that they are truly making positive change in this world.

Health in Harmony
https://healthinharmony.org/

International nonprofit dedicated to reversing global heating, as well as preserving and growing rainforest as this is essential for the survival of humanity. The organization is founded on Radical Listening, looking to the communities that guard the rainforest as the experts. The planetary approach, recognizing that humans, the Earth, and all creatures are deeply interconnected, is at the heart of Health In Harmony. Programs sites are in Indonesia, Madagascar, and Brazil.

Hope for our Sisters
https://hopeforoursisters.org

Women who advocate and raise support for women suffering from and at risk for obstetric and traumatic fistula in the DRC and Nepal. Women who acquire fistula from birth trauma are ostracized and lose their roles in society, so surgery to repair fistula is life-giving in that it returns women back to their families and communities.

Hospice Africa Uganda
https://www.hospice-africa.org/uganda/

Provide palliative care to patients and training for providers across Africa with a model clinic and homecare team in Kampala, Uganda. HAU is the manufacturing center for morphine in Uganda, where there would otherwise not be treatment for serious illness and end-of-life suffering.

Hôpital Bon Samaritan Limbe, Haiti
https://www.hbslimbe.org/

Full service hospital with outreach programs such as a special needs orphanage, Kai Mira, potable water provision for the town, vaccination program, and pre/post natal clinics. Surgical teams from around the world visit for specialty surgeries.

A Ripple
https://a-ripple.org/

Provide medical care and WASH (water, sanitation, hygiene) services internationally without charge and without bias. Our mission is to provide humanitarian assistance to disadvantaged and underserved populations, refugees, and displaced persons internationally.

Rotary International
https://rotary.org/

Mission is to provide service to others, promote integrity, and advance world understanding, goodwill, and peace through fellowship of business, professional, and community leaders. Every single country I have visited has had active local Rotary clubs making positive change in their communities. And domestic clubs support international sister clubs, making for a beautiful global network.

University of Notre Dame Haiti Salt Project
https://haitisaltproject.com/

Mission is to eradicate Lymphatic Filiariasis from Haiti and reduce iodine deficiency disorders. By fortifying salt with iodine and DEC, both of these objectives are addressed. Notre Dame produces and distributes this Bon Sel (good salt) in country.

Dr. Christina E. Fitch (aka Ina) has visited 35 countries, sometimes as a doctor/teacher, but always as a student of culture and spirituality. She is a proud Domer (Notre Dame alma mater). Professionally, she is passionate about Palliative Medicine, Hospice Care, Medical Education, Healthcare Systems, and Ethics in Global Health. Personally, she loves gardening, entertaining, kayaking, singing, and hiking. She is based in Connecticut.

Photo credit: Vella photography.

Green Heart Living's mission is to make the world a more loving and peaceful place, one person at a time. Green Heart Living Press publishes inspirational books and stories of transformation, making the world a more loving and peaceful place, one book at a time.

Whether you have an idea for an inspirational book and want support through the writing process – or your book is already written and you are looking for a publishing path – Green Heart Living can help you get your book out into the world.

You can meet Green Heart authors on the Green Heart Living YouTube channel and the Green Heart Living Podcast.

Made in the USA
Las Vegas, NV
16 December 2022

62718279R00095